SAVING LADY LIBERTY

JOSEPH PULITZER'S FIGHT FOR THE STATUE OF LIBERTY

CLAUDIA FRIDDELL

ILLUSTRATED BY
STACY INNERST

CALKINS CREEK
AN IMPRINT OF BOYDS MILLS & KANE
New York

J oseph Pulitzer loved words. And the word he loved best was *liberty*.

Maybe that's because Joseph, the son of a wealthy Jewish merchant, enjoyed freedoms that other Jewish boys outside of Pest, Hungary, could not. But after his father died when Joseph was eleven, his world changed forever.

Penniless from his father's death and his family's misfortunes, Joseph left home at seventeen to join the army. But no army in Europe wanted a scrawny teenager, nearly blind without his glasses.

Fortunately, President Lincoln's U.S. Army did. When Joseph heard that he could get paid to fight for the Union, he set sail—determined to make a new start in the land of liberty.

Proud to be a soldier in the First New York (Lincoln) Cavalry, the frail Hungarian was better suited for combat on the chessboard than on the battlefield. Bullied by his German-speaking regiment and bored with guard duty, Joseph couldn't wait for the Civil War to end.

But finding work in New York City proved tougher than serving in the army. Joseph might have been fluent in French, German, Hungarian, and Yiddish—but a poor immigrant who didn't speak English couldn't compete with thousands of other veterans.

After weeks of sleeping on park benches, Joseph hopped a train and headed for St. Louis—a city filled with German-speaking immigrants.

Joseph felt right at home in this river port city, even if he couldn't find a job he liked. He shoveled coal, waited tables, dug graves, and even tended stubborn mules!

But Joseph never minded working at the Mercantile Library, teaching himself to read and write in English. He especially didn't mind taking breaks in the chess room. Not only did Joseph's masterful moves draw a crowd, they drew the admiration of the owner of a German language newspaper.

When Joseph landed a reporting job at the *Westliche Post*, he finally had a job he loved.

Grateful for the freedom to write what he chose, Joseph uncovered corruption and inequality. His brash manner and relentless drive didn't earn him many friends, but no matter—Joseph kept moving up until he owned the newspaper alongside his chess-playing boss.

After selling his shares of the paper, Joseph had
money to spend and freedom to travel.

At the 1878 Paris World's Fair—a spectacle of the
world's latest inventions—Joseph and his new bride
were dazzled by Alexander Graham Bell's talking
machine and Thomas Edison's magical music box.

But it was the colossal copper head of Auguste Bartholdi's unfinished statue, *Liberty Enlightening the World*, that captured Joseph's attention.

Joseph Pulitzer shared Auguste Bartholdi's dream that one day, the sculptor's magnificent monument to liberty would stand in New York's harbor—the gateway to the land of opportunity.

But both dreamers knew that the French were more excited to give their gift of friendship than Americans were to accept it. The United States had agreed to build a pedestal for the statue on Bedloe's Island in the heart of New York's harbor. But even New Yorkers weren't interested in paying for it.

Pulitzer didn't understand how Americans could turn their backs on France, the country that had fought for America's independence. He returned home determined to rally his countrymen to pay for the pedestal.

When Pulitzer bought the *New York World* newspaper, he did more than just write about Lady Liberty—he put her smack dab in the middle of its masthead!

Big Dave Orr

Racing Horse

Mark Twain

And when he wasn't selling the news, Pulitzer and the pedestal committee hosted horse races, boxing matches, and baseball games to raise funds. World-class musicians gave concerts, and writers such as Walt Whitman, Mark Twain, and a lesser-known poet named Emma Lazarus auctioned off their work.

ohn L. Sullivan   Walt Whitman   Joseph Pulitzer   Emma Lazarus

Pulitzer printed "The New Colossus"—Lazarus's
sonnet of a "world-wide welcome" from the "Mother
of Exiles"—hoping to inspire patriotism among
other immigrants. But the pedestal fund still needed
$100,000 to get Lady Liberty on her feet.

In 1884—nine years after Bartholdi began building his masterpiece—Lady Liberty stood fully-grown in the heart of Paris. But the building on Bedloe's Island had stopped. The pedestal fund had run dry.

Furious, Pulitzer scolded the wealthy New Yorkers who hadn't donated a penny.

He warned them that if New York didn't accept France's gift of friendship, Philadelphia or Boston would.

The World

What a burning disgrace it will be to the United States if the statue of the goddess is brought to our shores on a French government vessel and is met by the intelligence that our people, with all their wealth, have not enough public spirit, liberality and pride to provide a fitting pedestal on which it can be placed!

But the millionaires ignored him. Even the U.S. Congress and the governor of New York denied money for the pedestal! Frantic, Pulitzer searched for words to inspire his readers.

WHAT SHALL BE DONE WITH THE GREAT BARTHOLDI STATUE?

There is but one thing that can be done. *We must raise the money!*
  THE WORLD is the people's paper, and it now appeals to the people to come forward and raise this money. . . . Let us not wait for the millionaires to give this money. It is not a gift from the millionaires of France to the millionaires of America, but a gift of the whole people of France to the whole people of America. Give something, however little.

If he expected his readers to give their hard-earned money, maybe he should give them something in return.

It was risky, but Pulitzer decided to make his readers a promise. If a person donated even a penny, he would print *their* name and *their* story in the *World*.

Pulitzer donated $1,000 and left the rest up to the people.

The next day, he received a few names, coins, and stories. In the days and weeks that followed, more names, more coins, and more stories of sacrifice and patriotism poured in.

Children emptied piggy banks, waitresses mailed tips, and poker players sacrificed jackpots!

While Americans rushed to read the donors' names and inspiring stories, the French bid *adieu* to their beloved gift.

It was time for Lady Liberty to make her journey to America. Loaded with 214 crates of the statue's pieces, the *Isère* survived a stormy start before making its way across the Atlantic. The *World*'s readers worried and waited for news of the ship's fate.

On June 17, 1885, cheering crowds
greeted the ocean-battered voyager as it
sailed into New York's harbor. But with the pedestal
only half finished, Lady Liberty had no place to stand.
Now that crates filled with her copper skin and steel spine
lay huddled on Bedloe's Island, Americans rushed to send in
their donations.

More than 120,000 people pitched in to raise $102,000. Young and old. Rich and poor. And, just like Pulitzer, veterans and immigrants. Together, they saved Lady Liberty.

Joseph Pulitzer had kept his promise. He printed every name and every story!

TRIUMPHANT COMPLETION OF THE WORLD'S FUND FOR THE LIBERTY PEDESTAL

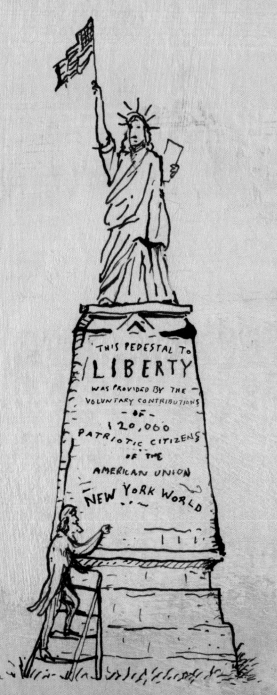

I sold two pumpkins and one squash at the market this morning and to show you that I am in favor of Liberty Enlightening the World, I send the proceeds of the squash and pumpkins, 10 cents.
— Mark T.

N.B. — I am going to make Farmer Emwrong sell some potatoes for the fund, too.

— Port Jarvis

I am a little spaniel dog. My master is very kind to me, but says he can't spare much for my account. I read your paper daily (that is, my master does), and I love "liberty" as much as most dogs do, even if millionaires do not. Please accept my mite of $5.

Truly, Your dog,
"Cio"

2 months later....

Your dog "Cio" finds he cannot attend Col. Knox's lecture tonight, and wishes you to accept his ticket money on account of Bartholdi Fund. $1 enclosed.

I am a little girl only eight years old. I send 10 cents for the pedestal contribution so in after-life I can say I did something towards its erection.
— Emily

I am a little boy six years old. Mama gave four cents, which I put in my frog-bank. I got three cents from Fannie, two cents from Claire, one cent from Harry. Please give the 10 cents to the statue fund.

— Albany, N.Y.

Inclosed please find $2 subscribed by the boys of the Hebrew Sheltering Guardian Society on a visiting day, for the Bartholdi Pedestal Fund, as below. Hoping the cause you have undertaken may prove a success. I remain.

— J.M.L., N.Y.

We send you from our kindergarten at Davenport, Iowa for the pedestal of Bartholdi Statue, $1.35. I am a little girl belonging to the school and am writing this letter for the school. We have twenty-six children at our school. I am not quite eight years old, and so you must not expect to get a very good letter from me.

— Esther

THE (i)NCLOSED 50 CENTS IS ALL WE COULD FIND IN SANTA CLAUS BANK WHICH PAPA OPENED LAST NIGHT. PLEASE GIVE IT TO MISS LIBERTY, WHOM WE HOPE TO SEE WHEN WE GO TO CONEY ISLAND THIS SUMMER, WITH OUR SHOVELS AND PAILS TO DIG SAND. I AM FOUR YEARS OLD AND SISTER IS THREE.

— YOURS,
JOHNNIE AND MAMIE

On October 28, 1886, Pulitzer stood in his office and watched nearly a million people parade under the arch he had built for Lady Liberty's homecoming.

It had been eight long years since Pulitzer first looked into Lady Liberty's eyes. Now, with his own fading eyesight, he witnessed Bartholdi unveil his magnificent monument ready to welcome every traveler with a torch of hope and a promise of freedom.

Pulitzer thought of Lady Liberty's journey and remembered his own.

Joseph Pulitzer had always loved words. And the word he loved best was *liberty*.

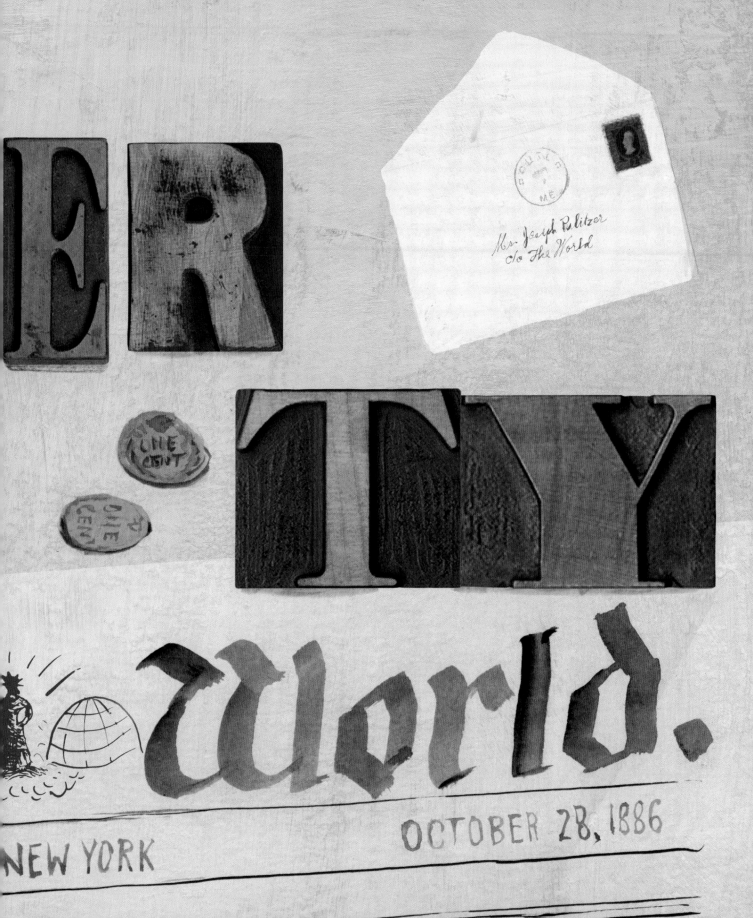

"I will always fight for progress and reform, never tolerate injustice or corruption, always fight demagogues of all parties, never belong to any party, always oppose privileged classes and public plunderers, never lack sympathy with the poor, always remain devoted to the public welfare . . ."

—Joseph Pulitzer

AFTERWORD

Joseph Pulitzer considered his successful pedestal campaign—the world's first crowdfunding effort—one of his greatest achievements. Because of his misfortunes as a child and his struggles as an immigrant, Pulitzer was driven to speak out against injustice and champion liberty.

He created the modern-day newspaper format, making newspapers more affordable, readable, and enjoyable for all people—not just the wealthy and educated. He added sports, entertainment, fashion, comics, human-interest stories, and investigative reporting pieces. He made articles shorter and more exciting. He added cartoons and illustrations to capture readers' attention. Pulitzer proved that good newspapers could entertain as well as enlighten readers.

Pulitzer's insatiable appetite for learning and his great respect for excellence inspired him to leave money in his will for the Pulitzer Prizes to reward the highest achievements of journalists and writers. He also left money to start Columbia University's School of Journalism.

Pulitzer suffered from poor health for much of his adult life. Four years after he watched the unveiling of the Statue of Liberty, Pulitzer was completely blind. Sightless and extremely sensitive to noise, Pulitzer spent his last years where he felt most at peace—on his yacht, *Liberty*.

LEFT: Joseph Pulitzer at age forty. ABOVE: In 1884, an exhibition was held to raise money for the pedestal.

FAST FACTS ABOUT JOSEPH PULITZER

• Pulitzer was rejected from British, French, and Austrian armies because of his young age, frail build, and weak eyes.

• Pulitzer was a self-taught lawyer, a Missouri state legislator, and a New York congressman.

• Pulitzer built a sixty-foot arch that spanned across Park Row in front of his newspaper building. The arch was decorated with French and American flags for the statue's celebration parade.

• Across the street from the *World* was one of the park benches where Pulitzer slept when he was homeless.

• Because of Pulitzer's pedestal crowdfunding campaign, the *World* became the best-selling newspaper in the western hemisphere.

The head of Lady Liberty on display in a park in Paris, 1883

FAST FACTS ABOUT LADY LIBERTY

• Lady Liberty has greeted over fourteen million immigrants who sailed into New York's harbor between 1886 and 1920.

• Édouard René Lefèbvre de Laboulaye, the French poet, author, abolitionist, and political scholar known as "the father of the Statue of Liberty," came up with the idea for a monument as a centennial gift to America. He shared his idea with Auguste Bartholdi during a dinner party at de Laboulaye's home.

• In 1875, Laboulaye founded the Franco-American Union Committee. Members from both countries helped fundraise for the statue and pedestal.

• Six hundred French artisans built the statue at Bartholdi's studio in Paris from 1875–1884.

• The statue was built in eight horizontal sections.

• The spine of the statue is a steel staircase built by Gustave Eiffel, the same engineer who designed the Eiffel Tower.

• Bartholdi's first model of the statue was four feet tall (the height of an average fourth grader). His second was doubled to 9.5 feet (an approximate ceiling height). He then quadrupled his model to thirty-eight feet (the height of a one-story building). Bartholdi quadrupled this model again to its actual height of 151 feet (over half of a football field!).

• Lady Liberty in Paris: Bartholdi's original prototype model of the statue is at the Musée des Arts et Métiers. An original model also stands at the Musée d'Orsay. The replica of Lady Liberty on the Île aux Cygnes (Isle of the Swans) in the Seine was a return gift from America to France in 1889 on the centennial of the French Revolution.

• Three hundred fifty pieces of the statue were packed into 214 wooden crates and were transported on seventy boxcars to the Normandy port where it was loaded onto the French navy ship *Isère*.

• Violent storms almost sank the *Isère*, the French navy ship that transported the statue to America.

Auguste Bartholdi (bottom right, without hat) shows a visitor how the statue is sculpted.

• Lady Liberty's right foot is stepping out of a broken shackle and chains, symbolizing emancipation for all oppressed people.

• Thomas Edison proposed having a large phonograph inside the statue so Lady Liberty could talk.

• The Statue of Liberty, originally planned to be a birthday gift for America's centennial in 1876, was finished ten years later in 1886.

• The hand and torch were finished in time for the Centennial Exhibition in Philadelphia. They were then displayed for five years in Madison Square Park where people paid to climb up to look out from the torch.

• Thousands of small models of the statue were sold around the world to raise money for the statue and the pedestal.

• The masons who built the pedestal were primarily immigrants. They threw handfuls of silver coins into the mortar before they set the last stone.

• Bartholdi chose Bedloe's Island when he first sailed into New York's harbor.

• In 1956, Bedloe's Island was renamed Liberty Island.

• Architect Richard Morris Hunt designed the Statue of Liberty pedestal.

• The pedestal sits inside the star-shaped walls of Fort Wood.

• The Statue of Liberty was originally a lighthouse (1886–1902) shining twenty-four miles out to sea.

• The statue and pedestal combined is 305 feet tall, the tallest structure ever built at that time.

• Made of copper, Lady Liberty was originally the color of a new penny. It took over thirty years for her to turn green.

• The copper sheeting that covers the statue is only 3/32 of an inch thick. The technique used to hammer the copper on the reverse side is called *repoussé*.

• The seven rays on the crown represent a halo of sun rays showing Lady Liberty's divinity.

• Twenty-five windows symbolize the jewels of the crown.

• There are 377 steps inside the statue and the pedestal.

• There is a door on the sole of the statue's right sandal.

• Lady Liberty holds a tablet with *July 4, 1776*, inscribed in Roman numerals.

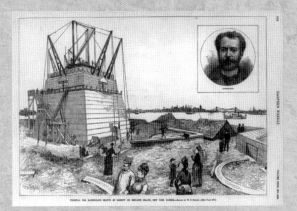

• New Yorkers voted to donate $50,000 for the pedestal fund, but Governor Grover Cleveland vetoed it. As president, Grover Cleveland led the dedication ceremony for Lady Liberty.

• Workers on Wall Street were the only ones in New York who didn't get the day off for the dedication celebration. When the parade passed below, the office boys threw rolls of ticker tape out the windows, starting the very first ticker-tape parade.

• Nicknames for *Liberty Enlightening the World*: Everybody's Gal, America's Freedom, America's Great Lady, Aunt Liberty, Bartholdi's Daughter, Giant Goddess, Grande Dame, Green Goddess, the Lady Higher Up, Lady of the Harbor, Lady on a Pedestal, Lady with a Torch, Mother of Exiles, and, of course, the Statue of Liberty.

JOSEPH PULITZER AND LADY LIBERTY'S JOURNEY

1847 – Jozsef (Joseph) Politzer (Pulitzer) is born in Mako, Hungary, to Fulop and Elize Politzer.

1848 – Revolution spreads across Europe and into Hungary.

1849 – Russian and Austrian armies overtake Hungarian army. Hungary's national customs and traditions are banned.

1855 – Joseph and family move to port city of Pest, Hungary.

1858 – Joseph's father dies.

1861 – United States Civil War begins.

1864 – After a childhood filled with loss—Joseph's father and seven brothers and sisters die from illness—seventeen-year-old Joseph leaves Hungary to become a Union soldier in America's Civil War.

1865 – The Union Army wins the Civil War in April. Only six days later, President Abraham Lincoln is assassinated.

1865 – Édouard de Laboulaye introduces at a dinner party in his home an idea to Auguste Bartholdi of a monumental centennial gift to America.

1865 – Joseph is honorably discharged from the army in the summer. After three months without a job in New York, he moves to St. Louis.

1867 – Joseph becomes U.S. citizen.

1868 – Carl Schurz hires Pulitzer as a reporter for the German language paper *Westliche Post*.

1869 – Pulitzer becomes managing editor and part owner of *Westliche Post*.

1871 – Bartholdi tours America to raise money and interest in his monument. When his ship arrives in New York's harbor, he chooses Bedloe's Island for Lady Liberty's home.

1872 – Pulitzer buys the *St. Louis Post* newspaper.
1872 – Bartholdi returns to France.

1875 – Laboulaye forms the Franco-American Union. Bartholdi begins construction of statue at his Paris studio.

1876 – Pulitzer becomes Missouri lawyer.
1876 – Bartholdi's artisans complete hand and torch. They are sent to Philadelphia for Centennial Exposition and then moved to New York's Madison Square Park.
1876 – Centennial Exhibition (first U.S. World's Fair) held in Philadelphia.
1876 – Alexander Graham Bell invents the telephone.

1877 – U.S. Congress votes to accept memorial gift from France. Congress formally names Bedloe's Island home for the statue. An American fund-raising committee is formed.
1877 – Thomas Edison invents the phonograph.

1878 – Pulitzer buys *St. Louis Dispatch*, marries Kate Davis. They honeymoon at the Paris World's Fair where he first sees Lady Liberty's head.

1879 – Gustave Eiffel begins design of the statue's steel framework.

1880 – The French people raise the $250,000 needed to complete statue.

1882 – Digging begins for pedestal on Bedloe's Island. Hand and torch return to Paris from New York.

1883 – Laboulaye dies.
1883 – Pulitzer buys the *New York World* newspaper and renames it the *World*. He fundraises for pedestal fund, attempts first fund-raising campaign in June.
1883 – Emma Lazarus poem "The New Colossus" is sold for $1,500 at Art Loan Fund Exhibition in Aid of the Bartholdi Pedestal Fund for the Statue of Liberty.
1883 – Construction of pedestal begins.

1884 – Pedestal fund runs out of money, building stops. Statue is completed outside Bartholdi's studio in Paris. On July 4, the statue is formally presented as a gift to America at a Paris ceremony.

1885 – Pulitzer begins first crowdfunding campaign in the *World*. After five months, his newspaper raises nearly $102,000 to complete pedestal fund on August 11.
1885 – The statue is packed up (350 pieces in 214 crates) and shipped to America. After nearly sinking in a stormy voyage, French navy ship the *Isère* arrives in New York harbor to great fanfare but an unfinished pedestal. Crates remain stacked on Bedloe's Island for over a year. Building of pedestal resumes after funds are raised.

1886 – The pedestal is completed in April. Statue construction begins. In October, over a million people attend the dedication parade (first ticker-tape parade) and unveiling ceremony for Statue of Liberty. Bartholdi unveils the face of the statue.

1887 – Emma Lazarus dies from cancer at thirty-eight.

1890 – Pulitzer, totally blind, retires from daily management of the *World*.

1892 – Ellis Island federal immigration station opens.

1903 – A bronze plaque with Emma Lazarus's poem "The New Colossus" is mounted to the interior wall of the Statue of Liberty's pedestal.

1911 – Joseph Pulitzer, sixty-four, dies on his yacht, the *Liberty*, in Charleston, South Carolina.

1916 – Stairs inside arm to torch are closed to visitors.

1917 – First Pulitzer Prizes are awarded as directed in Joseph Pulitzer's will.

1924 – The Statue of Liberty is designated a national monument by President Calvin Coolidge.

1956 – Bedloe's Island renamed Liberty Island.

1984–1986 – Restoration for statue's centennial birthday.

1986 – On July 4, President Ronald Reagan rededicates the Statue of Liberty for its centennial celebration as 1.5 billion people worldwide watch on television.

2019 – New Statue of Liberty museum opens on Liberty Island.

"If a monument should rise in the United States, as a memorial to their independence, I should think it only natural if it were built by united effort—a common work of both our nations."

—Édouard de Laboulaye

The inauguration of the Statue of Liberty on October 28, 1886. President Grover Cleveland arrived under a military and naval salute.

BIBLIOGRAPHY

All quotations in the book can be found in the following sources marked with an asterisk (*).

BOOK & VIDEO RESOURCES

*Bartholdi, Frederic Auguste. *The Statue of Liberty Enlightening the World*. Translated by Allen Thorndike Rice. New York: North American Review, 1885.

*Berenson, Edward. *The Statue of Liberty: A Transatlantic Story*. New Haven, CT: Yale University Press, 2012.

Burns, Ken, dir. *The Statue of Liberty*. [online.] Alexandria, VA: PBS Home Video, 1996.

Ireland, Alleyne. *Joseph Pulitzer: Reminiscences of a Secretary*. New York: Mitchell Kennerley, 1914.

Khan, Yasmin Sabina. *Enlightening the World: The Creation of the Statue of Liberty*. Ithaca, NY: Cornell University Press, 2010.

Mitchell, Elizabeth. *Liberty's Torch: The Great Adventure to Build the Statue of Liberty*. New York: Atlantic Monthly Press, 2014.

Moreno, Barry. *The Statue of Liberty Encyclopedia*. New York: Simon & Schuster, 2000.

Morris, James McGrath. *Pulitzer: A Life in Politics, Print, and Power*. New York: Harper Collins, 2010.

Thomas Edison video of the Statue of Liberty. Library of Congress. 52060 U.S. Copyright Office. United States: Thomas A. Edison, Inc. September 3, 1898.

Turner, Hy B. *When Giants Ruled: The Story of Park Row, NY's Great Newspaper Street*. New York: Fordham University Press, 1999.

NEWSPAPERS

"Commemorating the 100th Anniversary of Joseph Pulitzer, Founder of the *Post-Dispatch*, April 10, 1847–Oct. 29, 1911." *St. Louis Post-Dispatch*, April 6, 1947.

"Joseph Pulitzer Dies Suddenly." *New York Times* obituary. October 30, 1911. Reported from Charleston, SC, October 29, 1911.

*Joseph Pulitzer, retirement speech, April 10, 1907, *St. Louis Post-Dispatch*, April 11, 1907.

*Liberty Pedestal Fund and Statue of Liberty articles. *World Newspaper* archives, March–October 1885. New York Public Library.

"Liberty." The *Daily Times* [Richmond, VA], October 29, 1886, Page 1, Image 1, col. 3–5.

HISTORIANS, LIBRARIANS & EXPERTS

Jones, Thai, PhD. Herbert H. Lehman Curator for American History Rare Book & Manuscript Library, Columbia University.

Klapwald, Maurice. Assistant Manager Interlibrary, Document & Research Service, New York Public Library.

Moreno, Barry. Author, historian, and librarian at Museum Services Division, the Statue of Liberty National Monument.

Morris, James McGrath. Author of *Pulitzer: A Life in Politics, Print, and Power*.

ONLINE REFERENCES**

arthurchandler.com/new-pageparis-1878-exposition
digitalhistoryproject.com/2011/09/joseph-pulitzer-publisher-new-york.html
exhibitions.cul.columbia.edu/exhibits/show/pulitzer
gcaptain.com/statue-of-liberty-celebrates-130-years-since-arrival-in-new-york-spotd/
hdl.loc.gov/loc.mbrsmi/lcmp002.m2a01604
nps.gov/stli/learn/historyculture/edouard-de-laboulaye.htm
nps.gov/stli/learn/historyculture/emma-lazarus.htm
nps.gov/stli/learn/historyculture/places_creating_statue.htm
nps.gov/stli/learn/historyculture/pulitzer-in-depth.htm
nyc-architecture.com/LM/LM002-STATUEOFLIBERTY.htm
nypl.org/blog/2015/04/07/statue-liberty-pedestal
nytimes.com/learning/general/onthisday/bday/0410.html
nytimes.com/learning/general/onthisday/harp/0502.html
shsmo.org/historicmissourians/name/p/pulitzer/

**Websites active at time of publication

SELECTED CHILDREN'S BOOKS

Glaser, Linda. *Emma's Poem: The Voice of the Statue of Liberty*. Illustrated by Claire A. Nivola. Boston: HMH Books, 2010.

Maestro, Betsy. *The Story of the Statue of Liberty*. Illustrated by Giulio Maestro. New York: Harper Collins, 1989.

Mann, Elizabeth. *Statue of Liberty: A Tale of Two Countries*. Illustrated by Alan Witschonke. New York: Mikaya Press, 2011.

Rappaport, Doreen. *Lady Liberty: A Biography*. Illustrated by Matt Tavares. Somerville, MA: Candlewick Press, 2008.

Shea, Pegi Deitz. *Liberty Rising: The Story of the Statue of Liberty*. Illustrated by Wade Zahares. New York: Henry Holt and Company, 2005.

For all those who still yearn to breathe free,
and in memory of Guy and Gin Friddell—
newspaperman extraordinaire and his beloved muse.
 —CF

For my father, Ivan, who taught me to read the papers.
 —SI

ACKNOWLEDGMENTS

Special thanks to our expert fact-checkers Barry Moreno—author, historian, and librarian of the Statue of Liberty National Monument—and James McGrath Morris, author of *Pulitzer: A Life in Politics, Print, and Power*.

With gratitude for the privilege of working with Carolyn Yoder, for the assistance of Maurice Klapwald—Assistant Manager of the Interlibrary, Document & Research Service at the New York Public Library—and for the steadfast support from Rachel Orr, Rich Davis, Suzanna Banwell, Ann Matzke, Esther Hershenhorn, and Marcia Benshoof.

PICTURE CREDITS

Library of Congress, Prints and Photographs Division: LC-USZ62-41668: 40 (left); LC-USZ62-18086: 41; LC-USZ62-40096: 42; LC-USZ62-85641: 43 (right); LC-DIG-ds-04491: 46

The New York Public Library Digital Collections, The Miriam and Ira D. Wallach Division of Art, Prints and Photographs: 40 (right); 43 (left)

For information about permission to reproduce selections from this book, please contact permissions@bmkbooks.com.

Calkins Creek
An Imprint of Boyds Mills & Kane
calkinscreekbooks.com
Printed in China

ISBN: 978-1-68437-130-3
Library of Congress Control Number: 2019939440

First edition
10 9 8 7 6 5 4 3 2 1

Design by Barbara Grzeslo
The type is set in Akzidenz Grotesk.
The illustrations are done primarily in gouache and acrylic, with a little ink.

NOVEMBER 2020